year 5

The Word Bank

A picture dictionary for young readers

by Tony D. Triggs

illustrated by David Anstey

Nelson

Thomas Nelson and Sons Ltd
Nelson House   Mayfield Road
Walton-on-Thames   Surrey
KT12 5PL   UK

51 York Place
Edinburgh
EH1 3JD   UK

Thomas Nelson (Hong Kong) Ltd
Toppan Building 10/F
22A Westlands Road
Quarry Bay   Hong Kong

Thomas Nelson Australia
102 Dodds Street
South Melbourne
Vic 3205   Australia

Nelson Canada
1120 Birchmount Road
Scarborough   Ontario
M1K 5G4   Canada

© Tony D. Triggs 1991
Illustrator: David Anstey
First published by Thomas Nelson and Sons Ltd 1991

ISBN 0-17-432267-4
NPN 9 8 7 6 5 4 3 2 1

All rights reserved. No paragraph of this publication may be reproduced, copied or transmitted save with written permission or in accordance with the provisions of the Copyright, Design and Patents Act 1988, or under the terms of any licence permitting limited copying issued by the Copyright Licensing Agency, 33-34 Alfred Place, London WC1E 7DP.

Any person who does any unauthorised act in relation to this publication may be liable to criminal prosecution and civil claims for damages.

Printed in Hong Kong

Contents

In the bedroom	4 – 5
Time to get up	6 – 7
In the bathroom	8 – 9
Breakfast	10 – 11
In the garden	12 – 13
In the street	14 – 15
At the paper shop	16 – 17
The greengrocers	18 – 19
In the town centre	20 – 21
Building site	22 – 23
In school	24 – 25
In the classroom	26 – 27
At playtime	28 – 29
In the hall	30 – 31
Doing arts and crafts	32 – 33
School lunch	34 – 35
Finding out	36 – 37
Doing sport	38 – 39
Time to go home	40 – 41
At the hospital	42 – 43
On the way home	44 – 45
It's party time	46 – 47
Jelly and ice cream	48 – 49
Opening the presents	50 – 51
Tired out	52 – 53
Note to parents and teachers	54
Alphabetical word list	55

4 In the bedroom

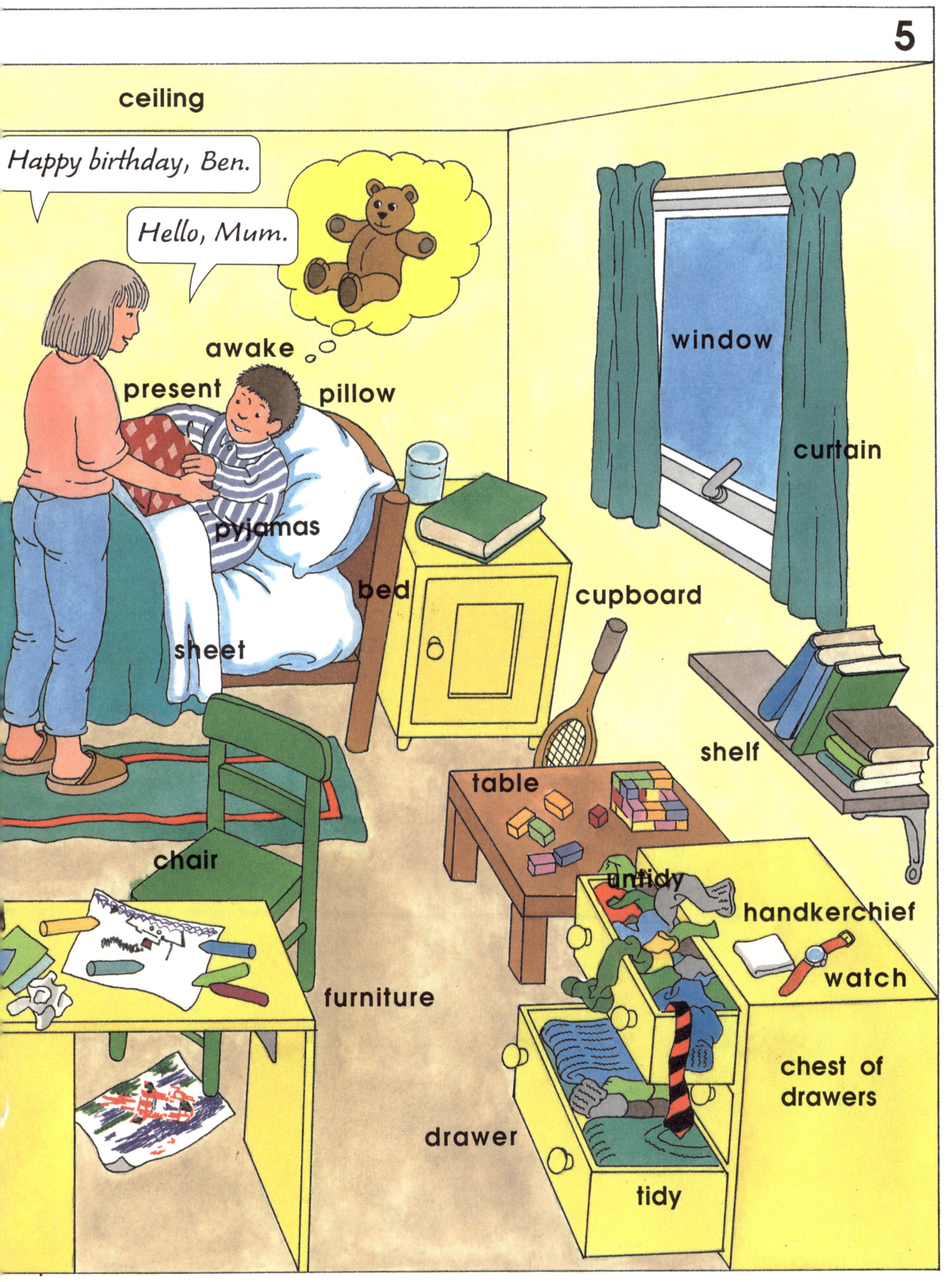

6　　Time to get up

Time to get up, Anna!

- clock
- doll
- mother
- bookshelf
- baby
- nappy
- cot
- car
- dummy
- duck
- rattle
- ball

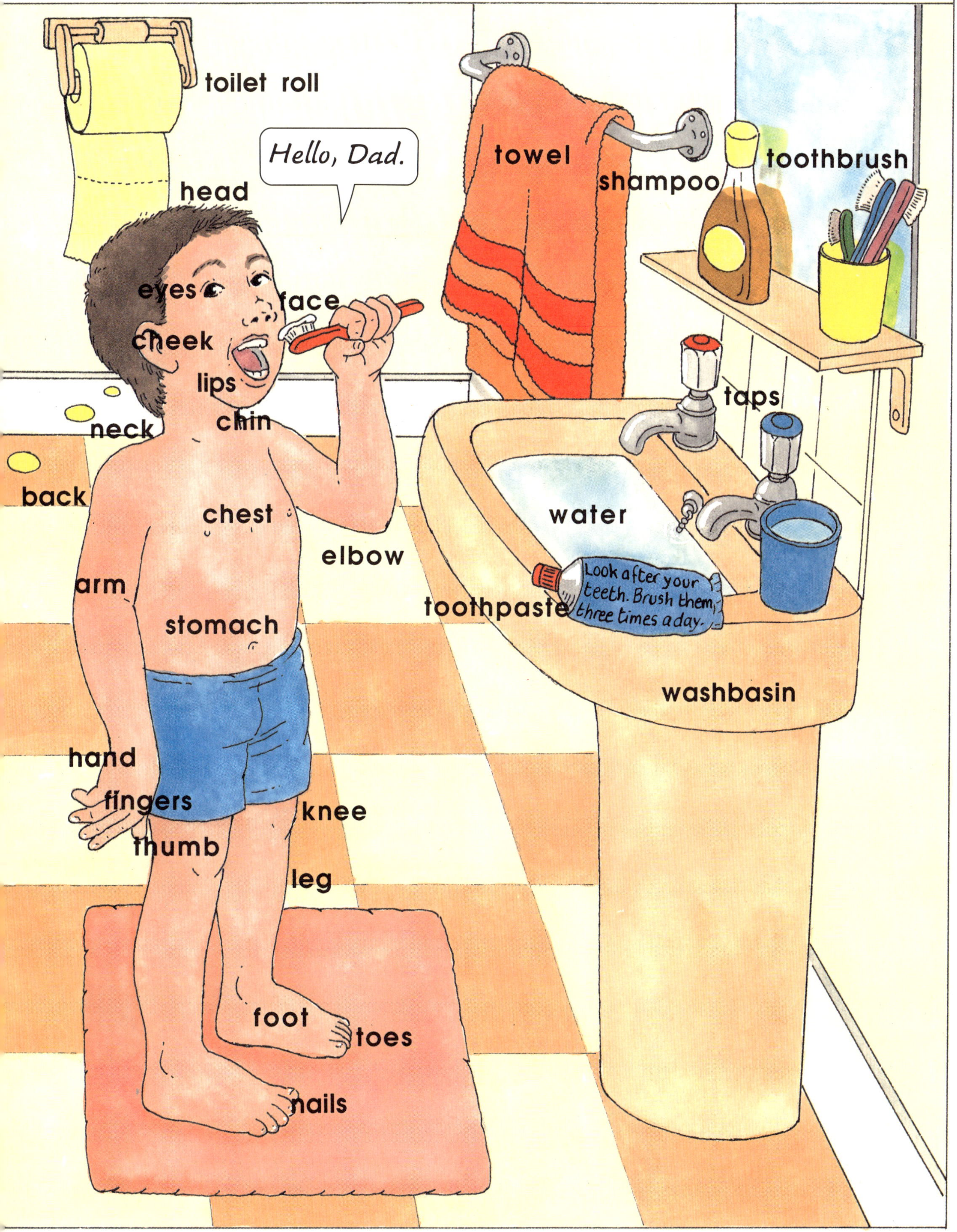

9

toilet roll

Hello, Dad.

towel

shampoo

toothbrush

head

eyes

face

cheek

lips

neck

chin

back

chest

elbow

taps

arm

water

stomach

toothpaste

washbasin

hand

fingers

knee

thumb

leg

foot

toes

nails

Look after your teeth. Brush them three times a day.

10 Breakfast

11

- clean dishes
- eggs
- kettle
- tea
- tea pot
- milk bottle
- tray
- washing powder
- bin
- jar
- washing machine
- work top
- egg cup
- eggshell
- high chair
- fridge
- plate
- mug
- iron
- pepper
- knife
- vacuum cleaner
- salt
- sausage
- baked beans
- ironing board
- fork

14 In the street

20 In the town centre

22 Building site

28 At playtime

postman
letters
rip
torn trousers

Are you Ben's sister?

We are coming to your brother's party.

fighting
crying
hitting
high
throwing
low
friends
ghost
witch
acting
eating
sweet
sour
dressing up

rolling
balancing
climbing
pushing
falling
hopping
flying
playing
waving

Happy birthday, Ben.
Thanks.

# In the hall

32 Doing arts and crafts

School lunch

35

36 Finding out

one o'clock

"Yes, it's gone red."

watching growing

"Does it change colour?"

weighing

heavy

light

asking

weights

telescope

microscope

"Oh, I can't do this."

pouring

trying hard

giving up

40 Time to go home

42 At the hospital

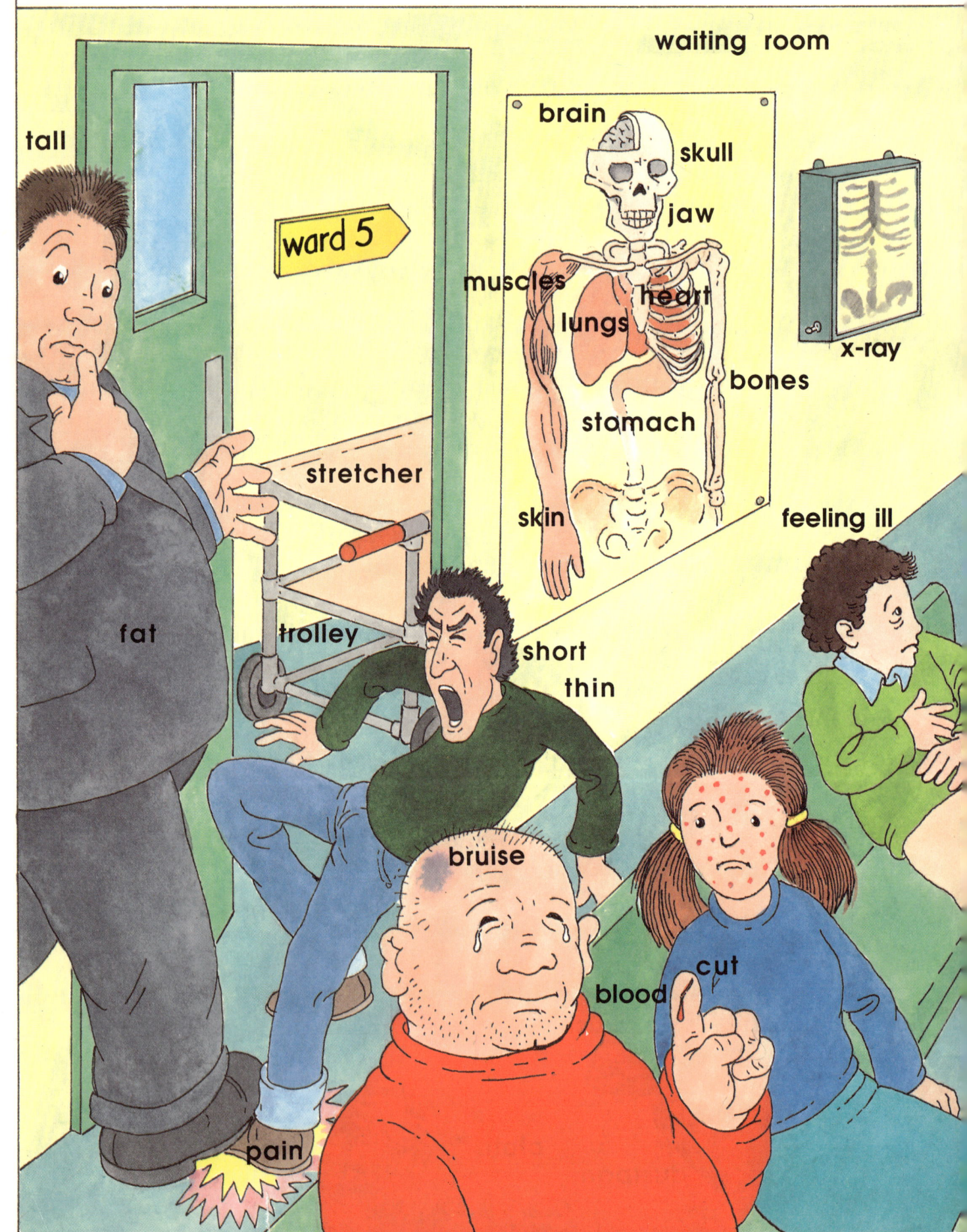

52 Tired out

Note to parents and teachers

It's Ben's big day! It starts like any other day but lots of surprises lie in store. A series of pictures shows us what happens, with objects, actions and characteristics clearly labelled as an aid to young readers.

Word Bank is not restricted by stuffy theoretical notions. It encourages whole word recognition but teachers and parents can supplement this with a phonic (or 'spell it out') approach.

To begin with, adults and children will simply follow the story by means of the pictures, and this can lead to 'finding' games as the adult names various features and objects. As confidence grows, the child can be asked to point to the labels instead of the pictures. Or the adult can point to the labels and ask the child what they say. A further idea is to show the child flash cards containing words from a chosen opening; the child can find each word in the book and 'read' it out. Up to this point the pictures have been the child's key to success; now he or she will start to recognise some words on sight.

Word Bank will be of value throughout the infant years. For example, the last two picture spreads, with their very few labels, offer the chance for more advanced practice and other activities.

The alphabetical index can be put to use in various ways. For example, as a child progresses he or she can be encouraged to practise referencing and memory skills. This can mean holding a word in mind while seeking it in its pictorial context.

Word Bank aims to make learning fun, and children should gain the satisfaction and confidence which are so important to early success.

Word List

a

accident 20
acting 28, 30
address 48
aeroplane 21
ambulance 21
angry 38
anorak 14
apples 18
apron 13
arm 9
armchair 46
arts and crafts 32
asking 36
asleep 7
assistant 17
astronaut 48
audience 30
awake 5

b

baby 43
back 9
bag 14
baked beans 34
balancing 29
ball 7
balloon 46
bananas 18
bandage 43
bank 22
basket 15
bath 8
bathroom 8
battery 16
beach 45
beans 11, 19
beard 8
bed 5
bedroom 5
bee 39
beetle 39
being greedy 49
being sick 43

bell 40
belt 12
bent 14
berries 13
bicycle 21
bin 11
bird 13
biscuits 49
black 32
blackboard 26
blanket 7
blood 42
blouse 13
blowing 37
blue 32
blunt 32
boat 45
boiling 37
bones 42
bonfire 22
book(s) 16
bookshelf 7
boots 15
bottle(s) 37
bowls 10
box 41
boy 14
bracelet 7
brain 42
branch 12
bread 10
breakfast 10
bricks 7
bridge 21
broken 37
brooch 7
broom 40
brother 28
brown 32
bruise 42
brush 7, 41
buggy 24
buildings 22
building site 22

bulb   5
bunk bed   7
buns   44
bus (driver)   20
bush   13
butter   10
butterfly   39
button   12
buying   31

c

cabbages   19
cakes   44
calculator   26
calendar   40
camera   46
candle   37
cap   14
car   7, 21
card   48
cardboard   26
cardigan   13
carpet   46
carriages   21
carrots   18
carrying   41
cassette (player)   47
cat   14
catching   38
cauliflower   19
ceiling   5
celery   19
cement (mixer)   23
centre   20
chain   20
chair   5
chalk   26
change   31
cheek   9
cheese   49
cherries   18
chest   9
chest of drawers   5
chicken   35

children   24
chimney   15
chin   9
chips   34
chocolate   17
Christmas (tree)   30
church   23
circle   32
clapping   31
classroom   26
clean   10
climbing   29
clock   6
cloth   37
clothes   5
cloud   15
coat   13, 15
coconut   18
coffee   10
cold   8
comb   7
comic   16
computer   47
concrete   22
cooker   10
cooking   33
copying   27
cornflakes   10
cot   7
cotton   33
coughing   27
counter   19
cows   45
cracked   37
crafts   34
crane   23
crash   21
crayon   26
crisps   49
cross   26
crossing (warden)   24
crying   28
cube   33
cucumber   18

cup 10
cupboard 5
curtain 5
curved 39
custard 35
customers 17
cut 42
cutting 32
cyclist 21

d

dad 41
dancing 30, 47
daughter 7
decorations 30
dentist 45
desk 5
dirty 10
dishes 10
ditch 45
doctor 43
dog 15
doing arts and crafts 32
doing maths 26
doing sport 38
doll 7
donkey 49
door 5
drain 15
drawer(s) 5
drawing 33
dream 7
dress 13
dressing table 7
dressing up 28
drill 45
drive 15
driver 20
dropping 41
drums 30
duck 7
dull 37
dummy 7
dust 40

dustbin 40
dustpan 41
duvet 7

e

ear 8
eating 28
egg (cup) 11
eggshell 11
elbow 9
empty 37
engine 20, 21
envelope 48
exercise book 26
eyes 9

f

face 9
falling 29
farm 45
farmer 45
fast 25
fat 42
father 8
Father Christmas 30
feathers 12
feeling ill 42
fence 15
field 24
fighting 28
finding out 36
finger 9
fire 22
fire engine 20
fireman 22
fish 12, 25
fish fingers 34
fish tank 25
flag 23
flames 22
flannel 8
flats 22
floor 5
flower 12

fly 39
foot 9
football 38
fork 11, 13
fridge 11
friends 28
frog 12
frying pan 10
full 37
fur 12
furniture 5

g

garage 15, 20
garden 12
gate 15
get up 6
ghost 28
girl 14
giving 48
giving up 36
glass 10, 22
glasses 8
globe 25
goal 38
goalkeeper 38
grandfather 41
grandmother 41
grapefruit 18
grapes 18
grass 12
greedy 49
green 32
greengrocers 18
grey 32
growing 36
grown-ups 24
gun 16

h

hair 8
hall 30
hamburger 34

hammer 22
hand 9
handbag 16
handkerchief 5
handle 5
happy 27
hard 22
hat 15
head 9
head teacher 24
heap of bricks 23
heart 42
heavy 36
hedge 14
helicopter 21
helmet 48
hiding 47
hi-fi 47
high 11
hill 45
hitting 28
holding 41
hole 22
home 40
hook 5
hopping 29
horse 45
hose 22
hospital 42
hot 8
house 14
hutch 13

i

ice cream 49
ill 42
insect 39
instruments 31
interested 31
iron 11
ironing board 11

j

jacket 13

jam 10
jar 11
jaw 42
jeans 44
jelly 49
jug 10
jumping 38

k

kettle 11
kicking 38
knee 9
knife 11, 35
knitting needle 33

l

laces 5
ladder 23
ladybird 39
lamp 7
lamp post 14
land 25
large 44
laughing 27
lawn 12
leaf 13
learner 21
left hand 49
leg 9
lego 16
lemonade 49
letter box 15
letters 26, 28
lettuce 19
lid 8
light (noun) 5
light (adjective) 36
line(s) 39
lips 9
listening 40
litter 15
little brother and sister 41
loaves of bread 44
loud 31

low 28
low notes 37
lunch (box) 24
lungs 42

m

mac 14
magazine 17
magician 48
making a model 32
man 14
map 25
market 44
marmalade 10
mask 43
maths 26
measure 26
measuring 26
medicine 43
medium 44
mess 41
metal 23
miaow 15
microscope 36
milk bottle 11
milk jug 10
mirror 7
mixer 23
mixing 33
model 32
money 31
moon 48
mosque 23
moth 39
mother 6
motorbike 20
mountain 45
moustache 8
mouth 8
mug 11
mum 41
muscles 42
mushrooms 18
music 30

n

nail(s) 9, 22
nappy 7
neck 9
necklace 7
needle 33
neighbour 14
new books 40
newspaper 16
nightie 7
nose 8
notes 30
notice (board) 25, 31
numbers 27
nurse 43
nuts 18

o

o'clock 36
oil 20
old books 40
old people 45
one o'clock 36
on the way 44
onions 19
orange 32
oranges 18
oven 10

p

pain 42
paint 32
painting 32
pan 10
pants 12
paper (shop) 16
parcels 21
party 46
passenger 20
path 13
patterns 32
pavement 14
peaches 18
peanuts 18
pears 18
peas 19, 34
pedestrian crossing 24
pegs 24
pen 27
pencil 26
people 14
pepper 11, 35
petrol pump 20
photographs 46
piano 30
picture(s) 25, 33
pie 35
pile of sand 23
pillow 5
pills 43
pilot 21
pineapple 18
pipe 22
pizza 35
plank 22
plant 19
plaster cast 43
plasticine 32
plate 11
playground 24
playing (the piano) 30
playtime 28
plug 5
plums 18
pocket 13
pole 13
policeman 13, 21
policewoman 21
pond 12
postman 28
pot 19
potatoes 19
pouring 36
present 5
price 19
programme(s) 31
pudding 35
puddle 15

pullover 12
purse 17
pushing 29
pyjamas 5

q

queue 34
quiet 31

r

rabbits 13
radiator 46
radio 47
railway 21
rain 15
raspberries 18
rattle 7
reading 27
record (player) 47
red 32
reindeer 30
repairs 20
rice 35
rider 45
right 26
right hand 49
ring 7
rip 28
river 45
road 18
rocket 48
rolling 29
rolls 34
roof 14
roses 13
rough 37
roundabout 24
rubber 26
rubbish 41
rug 46
ruler 26
running 38

s

sack 30
salad 35
salt 11, 34
sand 23
sandals 7
sandpit 12
sandwiches 34
satchel 14
saucepan 10
sausage 11, 34
saw 22
saying sorry 39
scales 19
school 25
scissors 32
scoring 38
screech 46
screen 48
screw 22
screwdriver 22
sea 25, 45
seat 8
seeds 12
selling 31
settee 47
sewing 33
shadow 48
shampoo 9
shapes 32
sharp 32
shed 13
sheep 45
sheet 5
shelf 5
shiny 37
ship 45
shirt 12
shoes 5
shop (assistant) 17
shopping bag 16
short 42
shouting 38
sick 43

signal 21
singing 31
sink 10
sister 28
site 22
sitting 30
skin 42
skull 42
sky 15
sledge 30
slide 24
slippers 7
slow 25
small 44
smash 38
smoke 22
smooth 37
sneezing 27
snow 15
socket 5
socks 12
soft 23
soil 13
son 9
sorry 39
soup 34
sour 28
space suit 48
spade 13
spaghetti 35
spider 39
spilling 38
spoon 10
sport 39
square 32
stage 30
stairs 46
stamp 48
standing 31
stars 48
station 20
stealing 30
steam 37
steering wheel 21

step 14
stick 17
sticking 32
stitches 43
stomach 9, 42
stool 7
stop 20
straight 14, 39
street 14
stretcher 42
string 26
suit 43
sun 15
supermarket 44
sweeping 40
sweet 28
sweets 17
swimming costume 13
swing 25
switch 5

t

table 5
tail 15
taking photographs 46
talking 40
tall 42
tame rabbit 13
tank 25
tape measure 26
tapping 37
taps 9
tart 34
taxi 20
teacher 26
tea (pot) 11
tearing paper 32
teenagers 44
teeth 9
telephone (box) 15, 46
telescope 36
telling a story 40
tent 45
test tubes 37

thief 30
thin 42
thinking 26
throwing 38
thumb 9
tick 26
tickets 31
tidy 5
till 19
time 6
time to get up 6
time to go home 40
tins 19
toast 10
toe 9
toilet (roll) 8, 9
tomatoes 19
toothbrush 9
toothpaste 9
top 16
torch 16
torn trousers 28
towel 9
tower 23
town 20
toys 16
tractor 45
traffic 21
train 21
tray 11
tree 12
triangle 33
trolley 42
trousers 12
trumpet 30
trunk 12
trying hard 36
tubes 37
turning the sound up 47
twins 43
tyre 20

u

umbrella 17

unhappy 26
untidy 5

v

vacuum cleaner 11
van 21
vase 19
vegetables 18, 34
vest 12
video 46
violin 31

w

wagons 21
waiting room 42
wall 5, 15
warden 24
wardrobe 5
washbasin 9
washing 12
washing line 12
washing machine 11
washing powder 11
wasp 39
waste paper bin 41
watch 5
watching 36
water 9
waving 29
web 39
weed 12
weighing 36
weights 36
wheel 20
whiskers 12
white 32
whizz! 46
wild rabbit 13
wind 15
window 5
windscreen 21
wing 12
wiping up a mess 41
witch 28

woman 15
wood 22
wool 33
work top 11
worm 13
writing 27
wrong 26

x
x-ray 42

xylophone 30

y
yawning 27
yellow 32
young people 44

z
zip 12